AIR BATTLES

Christopher Maynard and David Jefferis

Illustrated by
Terry Hadler
Ron Jobson and Michael Roffe

Franklin Watts
London   New York   Toronto   Sydney

First published in 1987 by
Franklin Watts
12a Golden Square
London W1R 4BA

First published in the USA
by Franklin Watts Inc.
387 Park Avenue South
New York, N.Y. 10016

First published in Australia
by Franklin Watts
Australia
14 Mars Road
Lane Cove, NSW 2066

UK ISBN: 0 86313 520 X
US ISBN: 0-531-10368-4
Library of Congress
Catalog Card No: 86-51552

Technical consultant
T Callaway, RAF Museum,
Hendon, London

Designed and produced by
Sunrise Books

© *1987 Franklin Watts*

Printed in Belgium

copy 1

AIR BATTLES

Contents

Introduction

This book is about the aircraft and air combats of World War II, which lasted from 1939 to 1945.

Germany, Japan and Italy were the Axis powers. They were opposed by the Allied countries which included Britain, America and Russia.

In 1939, many air forces still used slow and lightly armed biplanes. The pressure of war forced the development of many new technical ideas, including faster planes, powerful guns and airborne radar. By the war's end, jet fighters were in service, as were high flying bombers carrying immensely powerful atomic weapons.

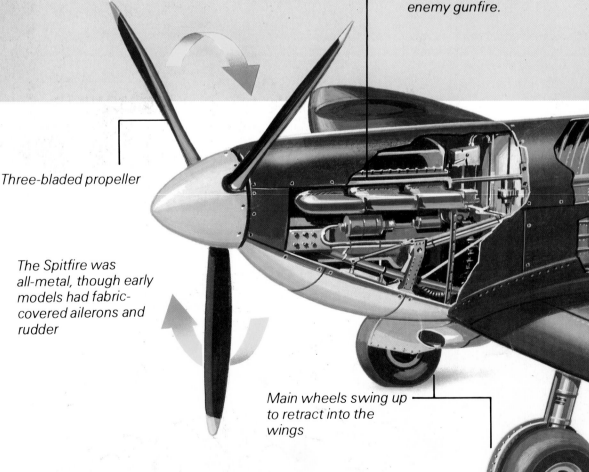

Powerful 12-cylinder Rolls Royce Merlin engine

Armor plate was fixed behind the pilot. He wore a parachute with which to escape if the aircraft was hit by enemy gunfire.

Three-bladed propeller

The Spitfire was all-metal, though early models had fabric-covered ailerons and rudder

Main wheels swing up to retract into the wings

Fighting planes

A new generation of single-seat fighter planes was developed during the 1930s. These were all-metal aircraft with powerful engines, armed with machine guns or cannon.

These streamlined, single-wing monoplanes had enclosed cockpits to shield pilots from the slipstream at speed. Top speeds reached more than 480 km/h (300 mph), but dogfights, using aerial maneuvers, were fought in much the same way as the air battles of World War I. Combat now needed more sky, although the shooting still took place at close range.

Some aircraft such as the Spitfire, shown below, were used throughout the war. Later fighter designs, such as the P-51 Mustang, were successful too.

Pilots were mostly young men in their early twenties. They had a little more protection than their World War I counterparts – armor plate in the cockpit and parachutes to escape with were standard equipment for pilots in most air forces. But the rule of air combat was still kill or be killed.

In World War II, command of the air was the first step to allow ground forces to take the land below. On every combat front, air control was vital for military success.

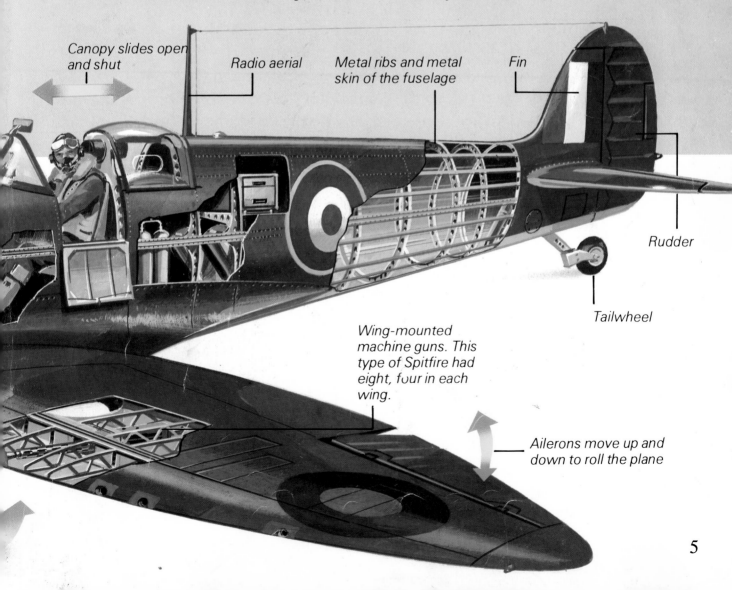

Canopy slides open and shut

Radio aerial

Metal ribs and metal skin of the fuselage

Fin

Rudder

Tailwheel

Wing-mounted machine guns. This type of Spitfire had eight, four in each wing.

Ailerons move up and down to roll the plane

Lightning over Poland

In the gray light just before dawn on September 1, 1939, with early ground fog blanketing much of the border area, German troops advanced into Poland. This was the start of World War II. Tanks and armored units moved forward on the ground. In the air, two huge fleets of 1,581 aircraft in all, including 210 fighters, raided far behind the Polish borders.

The German plan was to knock out the Polish air force while it was still on the ground. Using low-flying Stuka dive bombers, the Luftwaffe (German air force) hit ground targets such as airfields and aircraft hangars. This combined use of ground and air attackers was called "Blitzkrieg" – lightning war – named for its speed.

But the bulk of the tiny Polish air force of just over 300 planes (of which only 159 were fighters) had been moved to secret points well away from the former bases. The Polish air force survived the first attacks and, though badly outclassed, scored at least a dozen victories on the first day of the war. The Poles lost ten fighters with another 24 damaged. The main Polish fighter was the PZL 11c, an open cockpit aircraft that was slower and less well-armed than German fighters such as the Messerschmitt Bf 109 and Bf 110.

By the time Poland surrendered on September 27, 1939, 285 German planes had been downed, and roughly the same number badly damaged. But almost the entire Polish air force had been wiped out, with 234 aircrew killed or missing. Some pilots managed to escape to Britain, where they fought on in special Royal Air Force squadrons made up of flyers from Poland.

The Blitzkrieg was next used to conquer much of mainland Europe and, later, to advance across Russia. Early successes on the Russian Front were defeated by a combination of fierce Russian counter-attacks and bitterly cold winters.

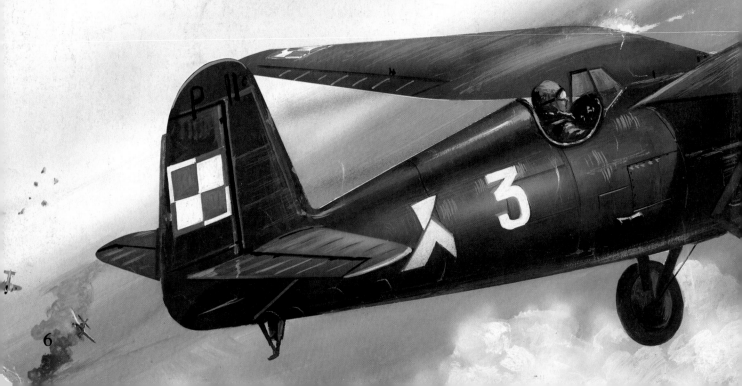

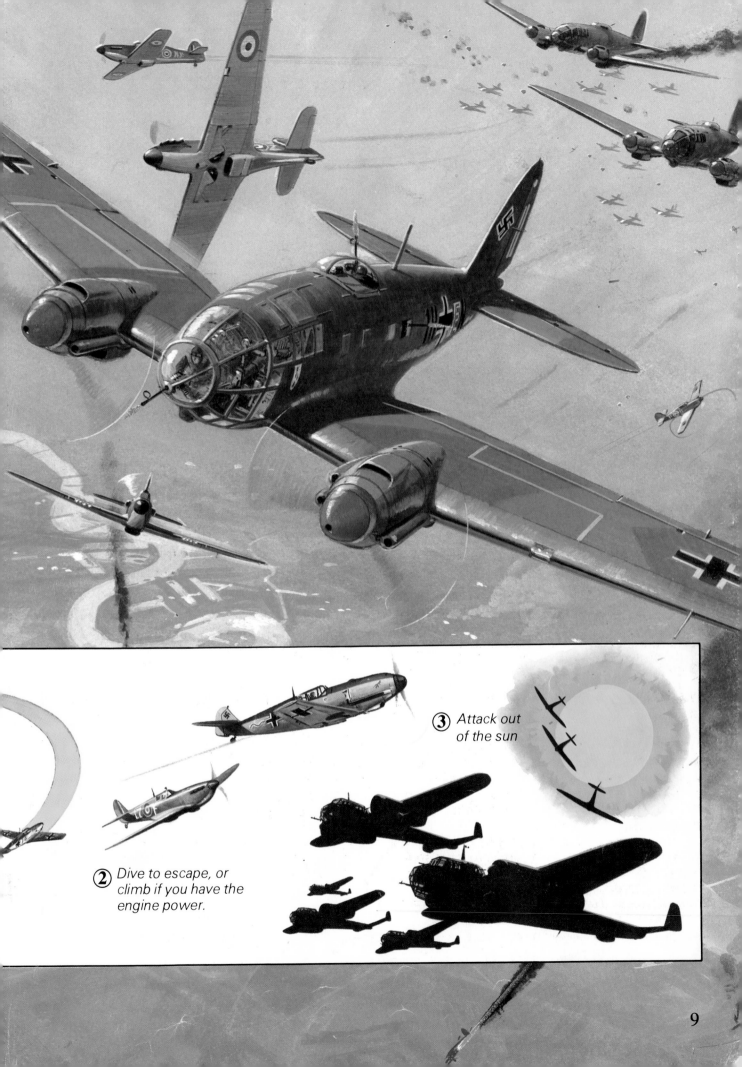

③ Attack out of the sun

② Dive to escape, or climb if you have the engine power.

Attack on Taranto

In 1941, the Allied and Axis powers fought for control of the Mediterranean Sea. The British navy had aircraft carriers, and the Italian navy's powerful fleet of six battleships, nine cruisers and 17 destroyers was moored in the heavily defended port of Taranto, in the south of Italy. Italian land-based aircraft constantly attacked British ships, but nothing could make the main Italian fleet put to sea. Without carrier-borne fighter planes for its defense, even the most powerful battleship was little more than a sitting duck for air attack.

In November 1941, the Allied

Operation Judgement was ready. This was a plan for Swordfish biplane bombers to attack the Italian fleet in Taranto harbor. At 8.30 on the evening of November 11, 1941, the first of 20 Swordfish took off from the flight deck of the British aircraft carrier HMS *Illustrious*. It was a mission from which few men expected to return. A pair of Swordfish flew high to drop flares over the harbor. These floated down on parachutes to show up the ships to the other pilots. The 18 other planes attacked in two waves, an hour apart. They were armed with a mixture of weapons; 11 carried aerial torpedoes,

the rest six bombs each. After a near-vertical dive, each Swordfish pulled out just a few feet above the waves.

The defenses were savage – records later showed that the harbor guns fired 22,239 shells at the 20 old-fashioned biplanes, flying at little more than 160 km/h (100 mph). The Italian target ships probably fired even more. Amazingly, only two Swordfish were brought down by the hail of fire. In part this was because they flew so low – once they were past the outer harbor, the Italians couldn't aim too low for fear of hitting each other in the crossfire. So, once under the umbrella of gunfire, the planes flew unharmed.

One of the last Swordfish back to

△ *The night attack on Taranto was not a complete surprise. One Swordfish arrived a few minutes early, alerting the defenses.*
The old-fashioned biplane, nicknamed "stringbag" *by its crews, could carry heavy loads of torpedoes, bombs, mines, and other weapons. Though a slow flyer, it was highly maneuverable.*

HMS *Illustrious* was one of the high-flying flare-droppers. The pilot was convinced he was the only one to survive, so intense had the battle appeared from high up. He landed to find most of his fellow pilots already aboard, welcoming him back.

The attack was a success and a turning point in the Mediterranean war. The Swordfish had sunk or badly damaged three battleships, damaged three cruisers, destroyed a seaplane base and hit an oil refinery.

Pacific air war

On December 7, 1941, 360 Japanese planes flew off aircraft carriers to carry out a surprise attack on Pearl Harbor, the American navy base in Hawaii. Four US battleships were sunk, four more were damaged and 247 planes were destroyed. The attack marked the beginning of a long war across the Pacific Ocean.

The aircraft the Japanese flew were better than any the Allies had at the start of the Pacific fighting. Among the best was the Mitsubishi Zero fighter, which could outfly any American plane.

When Saburo Sakai, a Japanese ace pilot first fought with an American Wildcat, a standard US naval fighter, he easily outmaneuvered it. Chasing from the rear, he approached to 90 m (300 ft), then opened fire, pumping over 500 rounds into the plane. He watched as the bullets chewed up the Wildcat's metal skin – but the 'cat kept on flying. A Zero, Sakai knew, would have disintegrated with that many bullets hitting it. The Zero had been stripped to the bone to save weight. It had none of the armor protection or self-sealing fuel tanks that American flyers took for granted. Though Zeroes had good performance, they could survive little battle damage. But the Zero's ability to out-climb and out-turn its opponents meant that in a straight fight, Zeroes were nearly unbeatable. Wildcat pilots used only hit-and-run

tactics against them – diving from above, firing, then zooming away to escape. Trying to dogfight with a Zero meant asking for trouble.

Not until newer types of plane, such as the F6F Hellcat, appeared in 1943 did US pilots have anything to match the Japanese fighter.

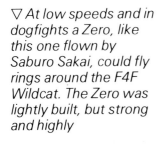

▽ At low speeds and in dogfights a Zero, like this one flown by Saburo Sakai, could fly rings around the F4F Wildcat. The Zero was lightly built, but strong and highly maneuverable.
Only when the Hellcat was developed did the Americans have a machine better than the Zero in practically every respect.

V-103

Kamikaze!

In a desperate attempt to sink more Allied ships, the Japanese formed the Special Attack Corps. Its pilots, known as Kamikaze (the Japanese word for "divine wind"), went on suicide flights to crash explosive-packed planes into Allied ships. They were most effective. Kamikaze pilots accounted for 48 per cent of American ships damaged and 21 per cent of those sunk in the 44 month Pacific War.

Battle of the "flat-tops"

Much of the Pacific war was fought from "flat-tops," the navy nickname for aircraft carriers. The Pearl Harbor raid was only possible because the Japanese had a powerful carrier force.

After Pearl Harbor, the Japanese expanded into China, across south-east Asia and the islands of the Pacific Ocean. In April 1942, things went less well for them. At the Battle of the Coral Sea, US carrier planes sank one Japanese carrier and damaged another. The Americans lost a carrier too, but the Japanese advance had been slowed.

In June 1942, the Japanese launched an attack on the American-held island of Midway. The idea was that from here, they could strike again at Pearl Harbor and force the Americans back to the coast of California.

The Japanese approached Midway with the mightiest fleet seen in the Pacific. They had 11 battleships, eight carriers, 22 cruisers, 65 destroyers and 21 submarines. They lacked only one thing – knowledge that an American force of three carriers, eight cruisers and 17 destroyers was in the area.

On June 4, Japanese carrier planes

▷ Soon after 10 am on June 4, 1942, 55 American Dauntless bombers dived in to attack the Japanese fleet. In a few minutes, they had hit three of Japan's biggest aircraft carriers. Later, more Dauntless dive bombers attacked and sunk a fourth carrier.

The weather was perfect for such attacks, with calm seas and clear skies. But the planes had to survive heavy anti-aircraft fire from the ships during their long dive from 4,267 m (14,000 ft).

attacked Midway. While the planes were back on their carriers rearming and refueling for another attack, American carrier and Midway based planes struck back.

Four Japanese carriers, the *Akagi*, *Kaga*, *Soryu* and *Hiryu*, were sunk, together with hundreds of aircraft. The Americans lost one carrier, the USS *Yorktown*.

Midway was the turning point of the Pacific war. After the battle, the Japanese were forced on the defensive. Allied forces started a three year island-hopping campaign. They used air, sea and land forces to recapture all the territory that Japan occupied in the Pacific.

15

Battle of the Atlantic

One of the vital Allied supply routes was across the Atlantic Ocean. Convoys of cargo ships, protected by naval vessels, carried food and equipment from the United States to Britain.

German navy ships, planes and submarines, called U-boats, tried hard to sink as many Allied ships as they could. In 1940 and 1941, the Allies lost more ships than they could replace. In May 1942, 91 British and US ships were sunk. U-boats were the biggest threat, as they could "shadow" a convoy, launch a torpedo and often vanish without being seen. However, U-boats had to surface often, to recharge the batteries they used for power when submerged. And this was when they were vulnerable. Allied planes joined the battle, attacking with cannon, bombs, depth charges and rockets.

One of the best anti-sub patrol planes of the time was a flying boat, the Short Sunderland. It was nicknamed the "flying porcupine" by the Germans, for its heavy looks and defensive fire-power. Takeoffs were often spectacular in choppy seas. Slowly the bows lifted as the outer engines raced to full power and the hull pounded against the waves. As the speed increased, the big flying boat began to plane on the waves and throw off a thick curtain of seaspray. Once the spray was clear of the inner propellers, all four engines could be opened up to full power. At 130 km/h (80 mph) the porcupine lumbered into the air. As

▷ As well as being used for patrol and attack, British Sunderland flying boats rescued many survivors from wrecked ships or crashed planes.

Here, the crew of a ditched aircraft await pickup and a mug of hot sweet tea aboard the four-engined "porcupine."

well as being a fine patrol plane, the Sunderland could alight on the water. In reasonably calm seas, the plane could pick up survivors of naval or air combats. In really rough weather, supplies could be dropped and rescue ships alerted.

The Battle of the Atlantic had no official "end," but by mid-1943, the Germans were forced to admit defeat. U-boats continued as a nuisance, but never seriously threatened the Atlantic lifeline again.

Throughout the war, U-boats sank 2,828 Allied ships. Of the 1,162 U-boats built, 785 were destroyed. Of these, most were sunk by attacks from Allied aircraft.

△ Planes of all types were used to attack submarines. Rockets were used as devastating weapons later in the war.

Target for tonight

Getting bombers into the air was a complex operation. A typical airbase in eastern England needed 2,600 people to support 40 or so bombers, often Avro Lancasters.

Six hours or so before takeoff, fuel tankers filled up the bombers' wing tanks. Meanwhile, out at the bomb store, armorers loaded up trolleys with bombs. The armorers' work could be very dangerous – on March 15, 1943, a 1,818 kg (4,000 lb) bomb exploded while it was being loaded into a plane. The armorers were killed and 11 Lancasters destroyed.

Other essential work included loading the guns, running up the engines, and checking the electric and hydraulic systems. Meanwhile, flight crews went to the briefing hut. Here they were told details of the "target for tonight," the weather forecast, flight plan and other information. They left the briefing hut to get dressed in warm clothing, essential for high flying.

An hour before takeoff, crews arrived at their aircraft. A Lancaster usually carried seven men – pilot, navigator, radio operator, bomb aimer/nose gunner, flight engineer and two gunners. The planes were parked at their dispersal points and, in winter, were cold and frosty or running with condensation. Then the engines were started.

Then the pilot slowly opened the throttles and the aircraft rumbled towards the runway.

Aircraft were parked at dispersal points, so they could not all be hit at once if there was an enemy air raid.

△ This is typical of the many airfields in eastern England during World War II. The bases were used for Allied raids on European targets.

▽ Fast Mosquito planes supplied photographs of enemy targets. They also flew at dawn to check on the results of the previous night's bombing.

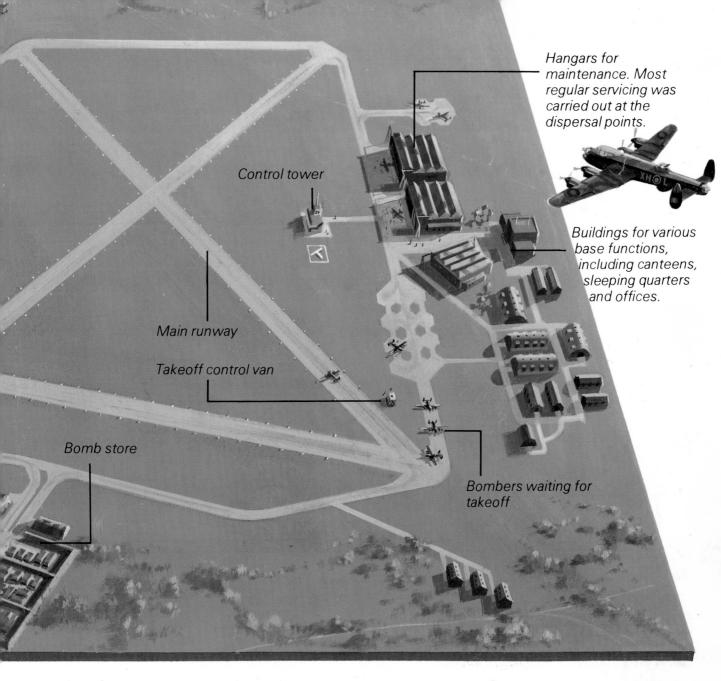

Control tower

Main runway

Takeoff control van

Bomb store

Hangars for maintenance. Most regular servicing was carried out at the dispersal points.

Buildings for various base functions, including canteens, sleeping quarters and offices.

Bombers waiting for takeoff

Small tractors towed bomb trolleys to bombers

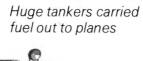

Huge tankers carried fuel out to planes

Crews were taken to their aircraft by truck or jeep

19

Night fighter

△ Airmen who parachuted into enemy territory tried to escape to friendly countries or were captured and held as prisoners of war.

By the end of 1940, the RAF and Luftwaffe had discovered that daylight bombing meant horrendous losses of men and machines. Both soon switched to night raiding.

In turn, night fighters were sent into action. The RAF used various radar equipped machines while the Germans had several successful aircraft, including the Messerschmitt Bf 110.

Wilhelm Johnen was a Luftwaffe ace who eventually made 34 night kills.

Late in April 1944, he was sent to patrol over the Nancy region in France where, soon after 1 a.m., his radio operator learned from ground control of an Allied bomber raid heading towards southern Germany. Soon, the Bf 110's radar picked up a signal at a range of less than 4 km (2.5 miles).

Closing in quickly, Johnen spotted the dark shape of an RAF Lancaster flying steadily through the moonlit night. Johnen carefully stalked his

The dam busters

Bouncing bomb

Dam

Reservoir

Bomb rolls down front of dam

Lancaster bomber

target but was spotted when barely 180 m (200 yds) away from the Lancaster. The bomber turned hard right with the Bf 110 on its tail. The Lancaster's rear gunner fired a burst – but missed. The Bf 110 dropped below and out of danger (a Lancaster had no belly guns), then edged upward.

Johnen fired straight into the bomber's wing tanks. Almost at once, flames began to lick the trailing edge of the wing. One after another the crew bailed out. Then the fuel tank in the wing exploded and the bomber, now a fireball, plunged to the ground.

On the night of May 17, 1943, 19 Lancaster bombers roared over Germany at treetop level. Their mission was to blow up the Moehne, Eder and Sorpe dams, which supplied electricity for weapons factories.

The Lancasters carried a new type of "bouncing bomb," made to skip along the water, roll down the face of the dams and explode 10 m (30 ft) underwater.

The pilots had to fly at a height of exactly

18.29 m (60 ft), otherwise the bombs wouldn't hit the target. Great skill was needed to hold this height, especially in the face of heavy anti-aircraft fire from the Moehne dam.

The Moehne and Eder dams were breached. Over 300 million tons of water cascaded into the valleys below. The Sorpe was damaged too, and the mission was a success. But the losses were high. Only 11 aircraft made it back to base.

Daylight raiders

In 1942, the American 8th Air Force started bombing targets in France and Germany from bases in England. This was part of the Allied air offensive which continued until the end of the war in 1945.

The number of bombs dropped was enormous. In 1942, 48,000 tons were dropped by the RAF. In 1944, the British and American total came to 915,000 tons.

One of the most used bombers was the American four-engined B-17 Flying Fortress, which normally carried a 2,724 kg (6,000 lb) bombload. When B-17s flew to targets in France they had fighter escorts. As the raids went further, over Germany, the fighters couldn't carry enough fuel to go all the way. Even so, the dozen or more defensive machine guns on a "Fort" could hose the sky with an immense weight of fire. It was thought that large formations of bombers could give each other protective cross-fire, to keep enemy fighters at bay.

In fact, unescorted bombers were very vulnerable. For a time it looked as if daylight bombing might have to be stopped. In October 1943, 60 bombers of a 300-plane raid on Schweinfurt in Germany, were shot down.

A real strength of the B-17 was the terrific punishment it could take. One American pilot told of being hit by a rocket, which took out a large part of the rear fuselage and tail fin, as well as cutting various control cables – yet his B-17 flew on and he made it home. Landings on only three and two engines were quite common.

Losses were heavy though, and long-range fighters were developed to

protect the bombers, including the P-47 Thunderbolt and P-51 Mustang. The P-51 could carry enough fuel for nine hours flying and could escort bombers on any long-range mission.

For all the destruction, the one real triumph for the air bombing campaign came in 1944. In April, the first of many raids was made against German synthetic oil factories. By September, the production of fuel for the Luftwaffe was down to 10,000 tons a month – and 160,000 tons were needed to keep flying effectively. Fuel shortages now became the Luftwaffe's number one problem.

▽ A damaged B-17 returns to its base. B-17s were able to absorb lots of damage, yet still keep flying.

Throughout the war, the Americans lost over 8,000 four engined bombers. RAF night bombers too took big losses. In 1943, Lancaster night bombers averaged only 40 hours flying time before being shot down.

Battle with the jets

In September 1944, airmen flying with the US 8th Air Force saw a new kind of fighter, the Messerschmitt Me 262. The Me 262 had no propeller, for it was powered by something new – jet engines.

With a top speed of over 800 km/h (500 mph) it was much faster than its opponents, such as the P-51 Mustang, which had a top speed of 703 km/h (437 mph). Jets were being developed in Britain and the USA too, but the Me 262 was the first jet to be used in air-to-air combat over Europe.

▷ Here, three P-51 Mustangs try to pick off an Me 262. The P-51 was regarded as a "hot ship" by Allied flyers, but it was far slower than the Me 262. But attacks could be successful.

The technique was to be at least 914 m (3,000 ft) above the jet, then dive on it and try to get in a burst of gunfire before the pilot opened his throttles to escape.

In this way two Me 262s were shot down in October 1944, by Mustangs of the 8th Air Force. Many others were destroyed in raids on their bases.

A standard Me 262 attack was to slip into position above and behind a bomber group. Diving, an Me 262 could hit speeds near 960 km/h (600 mph), flying past escorting fighters before the pilots had time to react. Leveling out below the bombers, the Me 262 pilot could then pick a target.

A dense pattern of air-to-air rockets might be fired. Packs of these could be carried under the wings. Otherwise, an ME 262 pilot could close in and pick off his victim with four powerful cannon, clustered in the jet's nose-section. The devastating punch from these guns could often make a bomber disintegrate in mid-air.

Fortunately for the Allies, Me 262s only entered combat in small numbers and far too late to turn the tide of battle. And most were used as light bombers, rather than as fighters. Had more Me 262s been available, they might have slowed or stopped the Allied air offensive.

The Me 262 was far from perfect however. It had a short range, only an hour's flying time, as the jet engines used a lot of fuel. And the engines, being newly developed, were not very reliable. They often failed on take-off, and could break up in flight. Engine failures accounted for as many losses as did battle damage.

The atomic bomb

The US Air Force B-29 Superfortress, named "Enola Gay," was warmed up and ready. Shortly before 3 am, on August 6, 1945, the bomber took off from Tinian airbase, on an island in the Pacific. The plane climbed into the dark, its target Japan, over 1,600 km (1,000 miles) away. The single six-ton bomb being carried was "Little Boy," the newly developed atomic bomb, with a power equal to 20,000 tons of conventional explosives. The Allies thought that using the atomic bomb would make a land invasion of Japan unnecessary as the Japanese would surrender when they saw the weapon's immense power.

The B-29 cruised toward Japan until 7.30 am when a coded message was received that the target would be the city of Hiroshima. A dawn flight over the city by a weather-scout B-29 had triggered air-raid sirens, but by 8.15 am as Enola Gay and its two companion planes flew over high, the "all-clear" had sounded. Nobody on the ground saw the bomb as it fell.

As Little Boy exploded, there was an intense flash of light, followed by a massive shockwave. Over the city a mushroom-shaped cloud rose. Enola Gay's pilot, Paul Tibbets, later described the explosion as looking like a boiling pot of tar, black and boiling underneath with a steam haze on top.

Under that haze, 71,379 people died, 51,000 were injured and 26 square kilometers (ten square miles) of Hiroshima were obliterated.

△ When the bomb was released, Tibbets pulled the B-29 away in a diving turn to escape the shockwave that would follow the explosion.

Little Boy fell to 550 m (1,800 ft), when it detonated over Hiroshima.

Three days later, another B-29 dropped the atomic bomb "Fat Man" on the town of Nagasaki where 80,000 people were killed. Within a week, on August 14, 1945, Japan agreed to unconditional surrender.

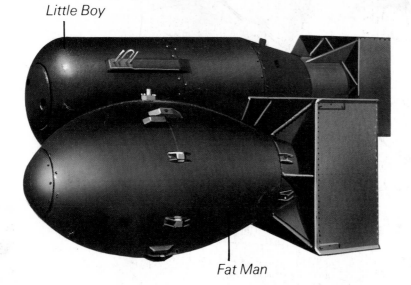

Little Boy

Fat Man

Little Boy and Fat Man

The six-ton Little Boy was an atomic bomb, equal in power to 20,000 tons of ordinary explosive. The biggest conventional bomb used in World War II was the British ''Grand Slam,'' which weighed 10 tons. Fat Man was dropped over the city of Nagasaki. The two atomic bombs brought the Pacific war to an abrupt end.

Aircraft data

Here are drawings of the main types of aeroplane described in this book. They are drawn to the same scale, so you can compare them in size. These were just a few of the many types that saw action during the war.

△ **PZL P11c**
Wingspan: 10.7 m (35 ft 2 in)
Length: 7.5 m (24 ft 8 in)
Speed: 387 km/h (240 mph)

△ **Messerschmitt Bf 109**
Wingspan: 9.8 m (32 ft 2 in)
Length: 8.6 m (28 ft 3 in)
Speed: 566 km/h (352 mph)

△ **Junkers Ju 87 Stuka**
Wingspan: 13.8 m (45 ft 3½ in)
Length: 11.3 m (37 ft 1 in)
Speed: 383 km/h (238 mph)

△ **Supermarine Spitfire MkII**
Wingspan: 11.2 m (36 ft 9 in)
Length: 9.1 m (29 ft 9 in)
Speed: 571 km/h (355 mph)

△ **Douglas SPD Dauntless**
Wingspan: 12.65 m (41 ft 6 in)
Length: 10.06 m (33 ft)
Speed: 406 km/h (252 mph)

△ **Grumman F6F Hellcat**
Wingspan: 13.05 m (42 ft 10 in)
Length: 10.2 m (33 ft 7 in)
Speed: 605 km/h (376 mph)

▽ **Hawker Hurricane**
Wingspan: 12.19m (40 ft)
Length: 9.55 m (31 ft 4 in)
Speed: 519 km/h (322 mph)

△ **Heinkel He 111**
Wingspan: 22.6 m (74 ft 2 in)
Length: 16.4 m (53 ft 9½ in)
Speed: 415 km/h (258 mph)

△ **Republic P-47D Thunderbolt**
Wingspan: 12.4 m (40 ft 9 in)
Length: 11.03 m (36 ft 1 in)
Speed: 690 km/h (428 mph)

▽ **Dornier Do 17E**
Wingspan: 18 m (59 ft)
Length: 16.25 m (53 ft 4 in)
Speed: 354 km/h (220 mph)

▷ **Boeing B-17G Flying Fortress**
Wingspan: 31.6 m (103 ft 8 in)
Length: 22.8 m (74 ft 9 in)
Speed: 462 km/h (287 mph)

△ Messerschmitt Bf 110
Wingspan:	16.3 m (53 ft 5 in)
Length:	12.1 m (39 ft 8 in)
Speed:	558 km/h (347 mph)

△ Mitsubishi A6M Zero
Wingspan:	12 m (39 ft 5 in)
Length:	9.1 m (29 ft 10 in)
Speed:	512 km/h (318 mph)

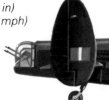

△ Avro Lancaster
Wingspan:	31.1 m (102 ft)
Length:	21.1 m (69 ft 3 in)
Speed:	462 km/h (287 mph)

△ Fairey Swordfish
Wingspan:	13.87 m (45 ft 6 in)
Length:	10.87 m (35 ft 8 in)
Speed:	222 km/h (138 mph)

△ de Havilland Mosquito
Wingspan:	16.5 m (54 ft 2 in)
Length:	12.5 m (41 ft)
Speed:	664 km/h (413 mph)

△ Grumman F4F Wildcat
Wingspan:	11.6 m (38 ft)
Length:	8.8 m (28 ft 9 in)
Speed:	528 km/h (328 mph)

△ North American P-51D Mustang
Wingspan:	11.28 m (37 ft)
Length:	9.83 m (32 ft 3 in)
Speed:	703 km/h (437 mph)

△ Messerschmitt Me 262
Wingspan:	12.5 m (41 ft)
Length:	10.6 m (34 ft 10 in)
Speed:	832 km/h (517 mph)

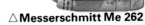

△ Short Sunderland
Wingspan:	34.38 m (112 ft 9½ in)
Length:	26.01 m (85 ft 4 in)
Speed:	330 km/h (205 mph)

▽ Boeing B-29 Superfortress
Wingspan:	43.1 m (141 ft 4 in)
Length:	30.2 m (99 ft)
Speed:	575 km/h (357 mph)

World at war

These two globes show the various places and countries mentioned in this book.

From the invasion of Poland in 1939 until the surrender of Japan in 1945, the war lasted six years.

But not all countries fought from the start. They were drawn in, one by one, over a period. The USA, for example, didn't officially enter the war until 1941, after the devastating attack on the base at Pearl Harbor.

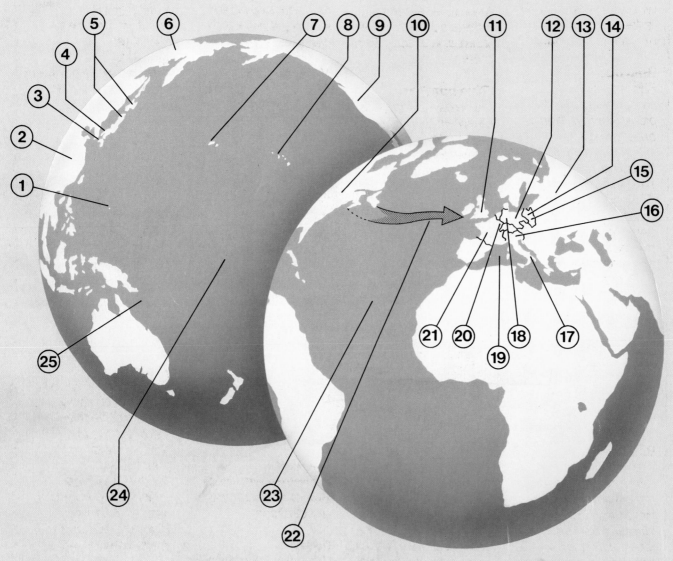

1 Tinian
2 China
3 Nagasaki
4 Hiroshima
5 Japan
6 Part of Russia
7 Midway
8 Pearl Harbor, on the Hawaiian Islands
9 California coast of USA
10 USA
11 Britain
12 Germany
13 Russia
14 Poland
15 Kracow
16 Italy
17 Taranto
18 Schweinfurt
19 Mediterranean Sea
20 Nancy
21 France
22 Convoy routes across the Atlantic
23 Atlantic Ocean
24 Pacific Ocean
25 Coral Sea

Glossary

Armorer
Ground crewman who loads aircraft with bombs and other weapons.

Atomic bomb
Extremely destructive bomb, the power of which comes from the release of the energy of nuclear fission.

Bail out
Flight term for parachuting out of a plane in a mid-flight emergency.

Blitzkrieg
The German word for "lightning war." Blitzkrieg uses planes, tanks and mobile troops to punch through enemy defenses.

Bomb aimer
Crewman who releases the bombload from a bomber plane. He usually lies in the plane's nose-section, looking through a special bombsight. He guides the pilot over the target before releasing the bombs.

Cannon
Powerful gun firing explosive shells.

Depth charge
Drum-shaped bomb dropped on a submerged submarine. Depth charges explode underwater to crack a sub's watertight hull.

Dispersal point
Area on an airfield where a plane can be parked, well apart from others.

Dive bomber
Plane able to dive at a steep angle, dropping bombs, then pulling out at low level.

Escort
Fighter sent along to accompany and protect formation of bombers.

Flight engineer
Crewman who looks after a big plane's in-flight systems, such as engines, hydraulics and electrics.

Flying boat
Plane with a boat-shaped hull that can land on and take off from water.

Hangar
Big storage shed for aircraft. Used for storage, repair and maintenance.

Kamikaze
"Divine wind," the name for Japanese suicide pilots and the planes they flew.

Machine gun
Gun which fires a rapid stream of bullets.

Navigator
Crewman who works out a plane's course and position.

Radar
Radio beam broadcast by a machine that can receive the "echo" bounced back from a solid object such as an aircraft. Radar stands for RAdio Direction And Ranging.

Radio operator
Crewman who keeps in touch with base and other aircraft using onboard radio equipment.

Russian Front
The German advance into Russia.

Synthetic oil
Fuel the Germans made from naptha, a mineral oil which comes from coal. The synthetic oil factories were bombed by the Allies toward the end of the war.

Torpedo
Cigar shaped "tin fish," several yards long. Has an explosive warhead and an electric motor for propulsion. Submarines fired torpedoes from tubes. Aircraft such as Swordfish dropped them from the air.

U-boat
Name for Germany's submarines. The name comes from "unterseeboote," the German word for undersea boat.

Index

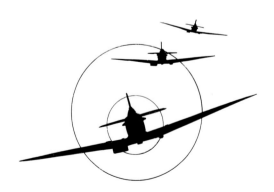

PRINTED IN BELGIUM BY
proost
INTERNATIONAL BOOK PRODUCTION